GOODBYE, TESTICLES!

A BOOK OF VERSE

BY

BARBARA BINLAND.   /2018.

ONE LONG CHAPTER: PAGES 1—81.

GOODBYE, TESTICLES!

This is one to read with your spectacles,

Some men seem to lose their testicles,

I am unsure whether or not,

To pity divorced men, or what?

Their ex-wives have them by the short and curlies,

So, what did you do to your loving girlies?

No, did not last long, sexy nighties,

It's called divorce, gives men a frighty,

And you have three ex-wives, you tell me,

Who has your balls, with your short and curlies?

AM I READY?

I sound androgynist,

Are all men misogynists?

Am I really ready, I ponder,

For chest hair, down yonder?

If you want anything done, I say,

Ask a woman, anyway,

I do sound androgynist,

Are all men useless misogynists?

Shall I ever be ready, I ponder,

 For chest hair down yonder?

MISSIONARY MAN!

Once upon a time of life,

I was such a loving wife,

Yes, he was a missionary man,

Only thing he could do, understand?

"Are we there yet?" I would lie and wonder,

Time so do some spuds for tea, is that thunder?

I have to get the washing in, you see?

Who else is going to get your tea?

In spite of this, I divorced the missionary man,

Is that all there is to love, understand?

"Shut up, brain?' I used to think!

My inner demon is a lovely chick!

THE BEST DAD.......

Here is some sage advice,

For young blokes, learnt from life,

The best dad is a great lover,

She'll be stripping off her covers,

Then you'll make happy memories,

 She'll be a happy old lady, you see,

A giggle in her nursing home,

" My old man was that big!" No moans,

So, she's still stripping off her covers,

 The best dad is a great lover!

MAKE YOUR OWN!

There is a new fad these days,

DIY is all the fave,

You can make your own,

Sex toys, that is, for fun at home,

Imagine lots of things,

Fave fun, with or without the wedding rings,

Be creative and look forward, I state,

What DIY sex toys can you create?

All you need is a good imagination,

Fun at home across the nation,

Yes, you can make your own,

Sex toys, that is, for fun at home!

INVISIBLE DICK!

Yes, it is good for chicks to have fantasies,

We can imagine invisible dicks, after tea,

Saves buying vibrators, you see,

And what are men, doing, anyway?

The single person, always a fave,

Inventing invisible dicks, after tea,

While boys gaze at bums and tits, prithee,

Portnoy's don't preach, you see,

We are not in bad relationships, I say,

Positive approach, that's the way,

Yes, it is good for chicks to have fantasies,

Or should we buy vibrators, one for you, and me?

A MAGICAL WORLD.......

Yes, it is a magical world,

For a proctologist, boy or girl,

They explore a nether region,

 For the greater good, a legion,

Had your prostate checked, lads?

For the greater good, no perhaps!

Yes, it is a magical world,

For a proctologist, boy or girl.........

SEX IN THE AFTERLIFE!

One wonders about eternal love, the afterlife,

What about if you were divorced by your wife?

Is there, indeed, sex in the overworld?

Or is it completely different? Asks an old girl,

What if we do not reunite in eternal love?

Can I take a bazooka to heaven? Not feeling doves,

Do women ever get to choose? I wonder,

Can, in heaven, I shoot my ex asunder,

No sex for him in the afterlife,

Not too much eternal love from his ex-wife.

COUNTING THE DAYS..........

Maybe the whole world is fatalist,

We half count the days to the apocalypse,

How many ways can we blow up today,

The human race and planet Earth on the way?

It's always at the back of our minds,

Seize today, that's my advice,

Maybe the whole world is fatalist,

Counting the days to the apocalypse!

RECYCLED SOULS!

Here is another old saying,

I hear some Grandmas stating,

As they gaze at their grandkids,

"Been here before....." do we take off the lid,

 Some kids are born, old souls,

 Recycled from heaven's abode!

OLDIES AND TECHNOLOGY!

This'll make you laugh, I know,

Imagine this scenario,

An oldie with technology issues,

Fixing it themselves, an a'tissue,

So they phone their latest grandchild,

Chatting on their smart phone for a while,

Toddler says impatiently to oldie,

Thinking they're a bit mouldy,

"Look, use any finger,

Press control A, then enter,

Easy, grandparent, easy,

Get mummy to bring me over to mend your PC!"

IT'S NOT EASY A TWEEN!

This is for kids in between,

It's not easy to be a tween,

Too old for kiddy fun,

Too young for teenagers' stuff begun,

You have to learn fractions and stuff,

You have to do homework--enough!

Never mind, kids in between,

It's not easy to be a tween.

NERD GIRLS!

Some chicks I know are pearls,

I think of them as the "Nerd Girls!"

They're all so hi-tech smart and savvy,

I wish they'd come to give me a wavvy,

One could live here, perhaps,

Save hiring some geek chaps,

Yes, chicks I know are pearls,

I think of them as 'nerd girls',

Nothing they cannot do,

Millenial girls are for me and you!

POTATO CHIPS!

Come on, woman, get a grip,

That was your last bag of potato chips,

One chip led to another, gone,

But their flavour lingers on,

Why not buy more, perhaps?

Because I'll be adding to my fat,

Come on, woman, get a grip,

Off to buy more potato chips!

DOING OKAY FOR NOW……..

This is an ode for all I know,

We're all a bunch of misfits, and so,

This is all I have to say,

For now, the misfits are doing okay!

CIRCLING!

Yes, we're all circling the sun,

Did you call me up for fun?

A man called me over,

Or was it all a big stir,

Or is it 'no immediate danger',

Are you my handsome stranger?

So, what was the agenda, sir?

As we circle the sun, are you a stir?

ORPHAN TRAIN........

These are days we hoped would never come again,

After the fascists' genocide orphan trains,

Tonight they're bombing the Middle East with our planes,

With chemical weapons, civilians don't wake in fright,

Yes, we're bombing Syria and Iraq tonight,

After Hitler and the genocide orphan trains,

Why do we still see these days again?

Shame, governments and extremists, shame!

SELF- SUFFICIENT!

This is for some women meant,

We grew up to be self-sufficient,

We grow into grannies self-reliant,

Reliable, kind, mini-giants,

But no one is ever really alone,

Even in separate parts of a home,

There's a power above us all,

"No one is alone!' the call.

HOW TO NURSE A GRIEVANCE.........

Yes, I must say emotions are so much fun,
Dare we say, quite normal for any human,

Nursing a grievance is even better,

So, I'll write my grievances in this letter,

My first grievance is politicians here,

They should sit down at 5 pm Fridays, dears,

And tell us what they do for the plebs,

Instead of barbecues with BS dregs,

Phony fear campaigns and paranoia,

Is this the way to govern Australia?

My second grievance is about hospitals,

Even for children, boys and girls,

On Good Friday, in Melbourne,

They beg in the streets from dawn,

Good cause, we all agree,

 Raise lots of funds, you see,

 Begging in the streets for charity,

In our great first world country,

Seems like a disgrace to me,

But our taxes should fund all this,

What are our pollies doing? Hiss! Hiss!

Yes, emotions are indeed quite human,

Nursing grievances is so much fun!

IF I COULD HEAL THE WORLD........

I want to be a helpful girl,

I really want to heal the world,

First, I would start in Australia,

So multiculturalism is not a failure,

I would dress everyone in a smile,

Then unify our great land, take a while,

No more bigotry or conflicts would be grand,

Racism is only skin deep, let's see some hands,

Then this is what to each I'd say,

"Don't let dickheads wreck your day,

Here is what you should all say,

"Centre your own f....ing chakras, eh!"

Then just declare, ""F....ing Namaste!"

Then I would give the world a bless,

"Whatever happens, do not stress,

No need for anyone to be drama queens!"

Is that the best advice you've ever seen?

I want to be a helpful girl,

I really want to heal the world!

VOCATION!

Here, in this suburban location,

I am sure I missed my chef's vocation,

This is a morning devotion,

Making breakfast with no emotion,

I am sure I could write a book of this,

I can cook stunning stale weetbix,

On Amazon , worth a look,

Winning recipes to cook,

Nouvelle Lucrezia, no need to sook,

I can also drown a teabag,

Not bad cooking for a fat old hag,

What is more than this?

After stunning stale weetbix?

Why, who wants some Imodium?

The chemist just sold me some!

Yes, with his morning cup of tea,

As I drown a teabag carelessly,

I do indulge in such cunning repartee,

Don't get dragged down by geriatricity,

I make breakfast with no emotion,

Here is stunning weetbix, true devotion,

I am sure I missed my chef's vocation,

Somewhere in a suburban location..........

THE VERY HUNGRY CROCODILE.

One night, by the light of the moon,

A little crocodile egg hatched, doom,

This will make you all wince,

Oz gave him to a little rich prince,

Yes, George's pal for a while,

A very hungry crocodile,

Growing up together, but speed dial,

This one did make us smile,

It was a very, very hungry crocodile,

On Monday, it ate a corgi,

Prince George thought it was funny,

On Tuesday, he ate old Prince Phil,

Prince George thought he was an old dill,

On Wednesday, he ate the queen,

Biggest melodrama you've ever seen,

On Thursday, he ate Camilla,

Prince George thought she was Godzilla,

This was a very hungry crocodile,

 On Friday, he ate all the corgis, with a smile,

On Saturday, he ate Prince George, tee hee,

On Sunday, he ate the rest of the nursery,

Then he ate the whole royal family,

So he wasn't hungry any more, you see,

That is how Oz got rid of the monarchy,

A feral pet from the 'colonies',

Comes from our convict ancestry,

 Thumbing our noses at authority,

 We do have republican tendencies……….

 This is how to get rid of the monarchy,

 Ha, is it a true story? Byeeeeeee!

GREAT GAMES FOR GROWING OLDER!
GAME #1. SAG, WE'RE IT!

Sag , we 're it,

We do look like gits,

Wrinkles are our funny bits,

No, girls, these aren't crocodile shoes,

They're our feet, aging's new rules,

 No, don't straighten our support hose,

They're our legs, that's how wrinkles, go,

Sag, we're it,

Nature's funny bits,

We do look like gits,

 Sag, we're it!

Game #2. HIDE AND GO PEE!

Hide and go pee,

This game is easy,

Don't go on long drives, tee hee,

"Where's the loo, and what's for tea?"

Incontinence makes this game easy,

Hide and go pee!

Game #3. SPIN THE MYLANTA BOTTLE!

Yes, time for Spin the Bottle,

Grandpas spin Mylanta at full throttle,

Got to kiss the nearest battleaxe,

Come on, dudes, down with the dacks!

Her grey hair matches her eyes,

Spin the Mylanta bottle, get a surprise!

Time for a new door prize,

Now who wants some Imodium?

The chemist just sold me some!

Game #4. MUSICAL RECLINERS.

Hit the music, girls and guys,

Musical recliners with a great prize,

First to recline,

Not to decline,

Gets free glass of Mylanta, yah!

Now ready, steady, today,

Musical recliners, make you pant, ha,

Now everyone gets free Mylanta!

Race ya, race ya, race ya!

Game #5.

Yes, baby boomers never grow old,

We're the ones who'll be hell in the nursing home,

It's time for zimmer wheelies, anyone can play,

Race ya to the lunchroom today,

Go, grannies, go grannies, go!

All in our support panty hose,

The nurses have checked our bowels,

Race ya to lunch, wheelies our vows!

Game #7. MEMORY BANK.

This one is a sign of old age,

A personal fave,

Found my keys, now where's the car?

I am sure it did not drive itself too far,

Now where are my specs?

Whoops, they're on my head,

Or did I sit on them instead?

Whoops, chatting on the phone today,

And by the way, what was your name?

Speak up dear, what did you say?

This game is Memory Bank, you see,

Now did I really drink my cup of tea?

A NURSING PLAN!

I know a very strange man,

Who is a nurse with a sound plan,

He is a gender queer human,

He tells folks to 'F…. yourself!"

Off to the drag bar, off the shelf,

Out of the closet for good, you see,

"F…. yourself!" a nursing plan for thee!

FOREVER YOUNG!

I practise observational methodology,

Studying folk in society,

I note octogenarians,

People I know of, like Willie Nelson,

They filled their glass of life up to the brim,

With bevvies, beers and gin,

These octos are full of vim,

Yes, over eighty, forever young, it seems,

Observing aging in society.........

BUT...... RICH!

As an old teaching femme,

I advocate literacy for women,

But I started reading Mills and Boon one day,

I must say they have really changed,

These days they are quite explicit,

They only have rich blips, and great tits,

Femmes only love billionaires, it seems,

White weddings, cat gets the cream,

With mistletoe engagement rings,

And anniversary twin sons, more bling,

Then renew their wedding vows,

Overcoming all issues, somehow,

This is the modern Mills and Boon,

Only true love with vast fortunes,

Maybe I'll write in this genre, tee hee,

Adding to femme's new literacy!

OLD TEACHERS!

Old teachers travel across centuries,

We have a lot to offer, you see,

We can sound like old Socrates,

Drinking his Hemlock for tea,

"Kids have no respect these days,

 Boys look like girls, except they shave,

Their music is total trash,

Their poetry is gibberish, that's that,

This comes from an even older age,

When Sumer appeared one day,

Old teachers haven't tanked it yet,

"Where is your homework, teachers' pets?'

Old teachers sound like Socrates,

We travel across the centuries,

We still have a lot to offer, you see,

And we have hides like elephants,

Enough of this, "I done me homework!" cant!

GENDER GAP!

Here I am observing,

Codes of life collating,

Men do dick things,

Femmes do chick things,

These days gaps are blurring,

Young gals can do anything,

But is there anti-discrimination,

Prejudice against males in our nation,

Or is it still the white male supremacists,

Appearing more misogynist?

Androgynists are sneering,

Still, men are doing dick things,

Femmes are doing chick things,

Emotions can be caring,

Love we could be sharing,

Here I am observing........

GUESS WHAT!

Hey, dear readers, guess what!

Is this a good day, or what?

I have declared, personally,

Today is a day of no calories,

Let's all celebrate,

Eat what we like today,

Enjoy varietal flaves,

Munching all our faves,

Fat bottomed girls, let's say,

Make the world go round again,

Start our diets another day.......

LIGHTEN UP!

Here's to life's loving cup,

We woke up, lighten up!

We're old and fat and grey,

We made it again, hooray!

Yah, we got so fat and old,

Now lighten up, don't whinge and scold,

Let's raise life's loving cup,

We woke up, now lighten up,

 Yes, look at each other and grin,

 "The assassins have failed again!"

ANY -ISM'LL DO!

We live in a world of 'isms',

Positivism, negativism,

Catholicism, Communism,

Optimism, or futilism,

Guess they're all cause for criticism,

Or that pure cynicism?

Which is, indeed, another 'ism',

Like atheism, agnosticism,

Theism, deism, or just cynicism,

Yes, all up for criticism,

Whoops, another '-ism'!

A NEW OLD AGE!

Is this what aging meant?

Collecting seniors' moments,

Reflecting on our long ago past,

Embracing each day as if it's the last,

No, baby boomers don't wanna get old,

Not like our folks did, be told,

We'll be causing hell in our nursing homes,

We're still driving our wheels,

Still learning new skills for real,

Debunking a digital world,

Golden oldies'll give anything a whirl,

Sometimes rest is best, okay,

Then we'll race around another day,

This is our new old age,

Baby boomers do turn the page,

To you, we'll leave our legacy,

Of growing old disgracefully!

BINNING!

Life in middle suburbia,

A little tale to bemuse ya,

Once there was a bin man,

Ordinary pot-bellied human,

In dork shorts, grey socks,

A good ole Australian jock,

He oft stated to his wife, you see,

"Leave the bins, I'll do 'em!" says he,

All those years, she did the bins,

Somewhere in a suburb of sin,

Mrs. Binnie got over that,

So she left him with his bins, tit for tat,

Now there's no one to get his tea,

Only a pot-belly bloke, in front of the TV,

"Leave the bins, I'll do 'em!' says he,

So she did, now he does his own bins, finally!

EMACIATION!

Here across this great nation,

Let's hear it for home emaciation,

I look after a geriatric, you see,

Save his family of F......ing C's,

Donate meat pies generously,

Signed, one of life's fatsies,

Now for choccies for degustation,

Let's hear it for emaciation!

EVERYONE POOPS!

Here is a thought for you today,

Everyone poops, let's say,

If you don't poop, you're in deep blip,

Everyone poops, don't be hypocrites!

RAISE IT!

Here is one suggestion for you,

How can we all raise our IQ?

Maybe by food as medicine,

Your body is what you' re putting in,

Yes, our bodies are temples, I say,

You can think better each day,

Reduce all those additives,

Enable all your digestives,

Maybe we can all raise our IQ,

Food as medicine, good for you!

FROM WITHIN………

Here is a tale from a world of sin,

From inmates at our big prison,

A simple tale, sad, but true,

Everything they ever wanted to do,

Was illegal, boo hoo hoo,

That is why they are in,

A sordid tale from a world of sin!

DON'T......

Don't take things too seriously,

Some people channel negativity,

Don't take it all too seriously,

Some people approach life so heavily,

They're in the glum fraternity,

Keep on smiling anyway,

These are our golden years, yah!

No need for any tears today!

NANNYVILLE!

Here I sit, I nurture,

A witch defining her future,

I convene Nannyville, you see,

Dreadful woman, but good for me!

Maintaining giggleosity,

I'm full of reliability,

As we demystify our aging, prithee,

Debunking myths about the elderly,

Yes, women my age do nurture,

This witch gazes at her future........

A BLAST FROM THE PAST..........

This is a blast from the past,

A true tale, laugh at chaff,

This is one of my gifts—nostalgia,

My GP once owned a piranha!

It ate the fish tank residents,

Trips to the butcher's , what this meant,

Long ago, and far away,

In a middle Melbourne younger age,

The tank was full of slime,

Piranha swam there, did its time,

Health and Safety got him a beauty,

Dr. flushed old fish down the loo, his duty,

Is the piranha still in the sewers? I ask,

How big did it grow? Its task,

Did it ever meet a Mrs. Piranha?

Tis one of my gifts—nostalgia!

MALNUTRITION VILLA!

We dwell here in suburbia,

In malnutrition villa!

Double chins so inviting,

Our cellulite delighting,

Nearly time for nosh bags,

What's for tea? Do we sag?

Yes, here dwelling in suburbia,

Cooking food for malnutrition villa!

GOLD, GIRLS, GOLD!

Yes, it's competition time,

I commemorate in rhyme,

Let all golden girls celebrate,

Oz swimming team girls, great!

Gold, girls, gold!

Hope you never grow old,

This idea is fun,

Now footy season has begun,

How to make my team number one?

I'll send for the golden girls,

They'd give the premiership a twirl,

Gold, girls, golden girls!

Oz swim team, gold, girls, gold!

Hope you never grow old!

SCOUT'S HONOUR.

Here is a story we hear more of today,

Scout's honour got lost along the way,

Boys all alone in the night,

Some scoutmasters gave them a fright,

Not so funny, paedophiles,

Alone with a spider for a while,

Here is a story we hear more of today,

Scout's honour got lost along the way………

WHY?

Oh, look, John and Betty,

Here is your tipsy mummy,

Yes, it is wine o'clock,

This'll give her kids a shock,

"Why are you tipsy, mummy?"

"I drinks cause you're bad, dummies!"

ARE MEN HUMAN?

This is a good question, sensitive,

Are men human? Their prerogative,

To think with their dicks,

Whereas we are the chicks,

Getting on with things,

Don't mean to sound misadrogynist,

Maybe I only know the manipulative,

It's nice to fantasise, about a male sincere,

Not much chance of meeting him here!

INTERNATIONAL DIALOGUE!

We gape at our world's glittering stage,

International dialogue needed for a new page,

We got what we voted for, what else to say?

All posturing on our world's giant stage…….

FELLOW FAGS!

Do I get mixed up with weirdos, or what?

Some males seem to lose the plot,

One dances around in bras and knickers,

Despite society's subtle snickers,

We must tolerate diversity,

Anything goes these days, you see,

I am frocked in male fleecies,

In that lingerie, I would look creepy,

So, am I a good boy, fellow fags?

Not my cup of tea, bisexual chicks and chaps,

But we have to tolerate diversity,

Anything goes these days, you see!

WHAT I KNOW!

Here is something I do know,

I read a book long ago,

"What men know about women!' I laughed,

Totally blank pages, not even a word of male chaff!

GANGSTER GRANNIES!

Are they all a bunch of twits,

Or merely cunning geriatrics?

Scared to the max,

Of being in aged care, rats!

Gangster grannies are really bitchfaces,

They have run life's races,

And old men, master manipulators,

In their BS, do not be participators!

UP IN THE TREE AGAIN!

One day, way back when,

An ape stood up, then,

Musculoskeletal issues for generations,

For thousands of years, every nation,

So, do we resume life in the trees, again?

Become bipedal quadrupeds, like way back when,

Yes, up in the trees again,

Would that be progress, or regression?

LET'S FIND OUT!

Let's find out, I say,

What is in your pants, today?

What would your wife say?

If we showed them something along the way,

Really teach them a few tricks,

Now do you really call that a dick?

Today I do not fraternise,

But it is nice to fantasise,

Roots are fun, you hicks,

Hope you all enjoy that trip!

QUIET GIRLS!

Yes, quiet girls are 'good girls',

Lots of quiet girls are in the world,

We have our own perversion,

Amuse ourselves with diversions,

Shhh, it is all a secret, you see,

Quiet girls have all the mysteries........

EX—CHICKS!

This is a special ode,

Didn't take me too long to compose,

One for all the world's ex-chicks,

For all you erstwhile hicks,

Hear the summons from the ex-chicks,

This is it, "Off with their dicks!"

Yes, boys, ex-chicks do understand,

 "You're not even an excuse for a man!"

"Off with their dicks!" the ex-chicks' plan!

FRIEND TO FUR!

When in doubt, pat a fur,

Most chaff is all a stir,

So, keep calm, pat a fur,

He gazes at me, eyes a deux,

When in doubt, pat a fur!

LEGALESE!

Everyone gives free advice,

Disregard to trash, don't think twice,

Bush lawyers and their legalese,

I know a real one, if you please,

Just don't open your big fat gob,

Or he'll shove his fist down it, you slob!

Or to nuisance callers on the phone,

"You f*** off my telephone!"

This is how to talk to perps,

Legal fist down gob, your desserts!

Solicitor on board for free advice,

All else disregard, don't think twice!

CHEAP THERAPY!

Ah, it's a misogynist rule,

But would a 'cheap slut' root you?

No, after cheap therapy,

We raise our expectations after thee,

Let's hear it from the women's world,

"You can go without!" of wisdom, a pearl,

Stop hanging back, like a jib,

Get someone else, or can't you, you pig!

DUST!

Dust, if you must,

Of do we reshuffle the dust?

Why this housework thrust?

Turn around, don't look, you'll bust,

I just reshuffled the dust,

Yes, dust if you must!

I TURNED INTO GRANDPA!

This is a verse to thrill ya!

I turned into my old Grandpa,

Self-limiting thoughts, you see,

Wasted on a bunch of F..........C....s!

NEVER ASK OUR MUM!

Here's a tip optimum,

Never ask our mum,

She'd say, "Wait until your dad gets home!"

Then chatter on the telephone,

"Now you clean off this plate!"

No leaving the table, even if late,

"No, can't afford that!"

"Make do, or go without!"

"Stop snacking, you're way too stout!"

Here's a tip optimum,

We never asked our mum!

RELATIVES!

Here is a new missive,

Old, but true, about relatives,

You can choose your friends,

But some relatives are round the bend,

No, you cannot choose your relatives,

Just as well, my new missive!

DEFINITELY BLIND!

Yes, love is blind,

Definitely! It lags behind,

Good sense and taste, when,

He taught me about fake friends,

Credibility zero,

No urban hero,

Good taste lagged behind,

Love is definitely blind!

LYRIC---MY VALENTINE......

I wish to grow old disgracefully,

But I invented a lover imaginary,

It is good for women to have fantasies,

I love you across time and centuries,

My thoughts are filled with such delights,

It does pass these hot summer nights,

I rouse myself from afterglow,

All in the head, this I know,

One day, I shall sit down and laugh,

With a good coffee, at all this chaff,

I did but see you passing by,

I sit and ponder, and heave a sigh,

Here's what I say to you, young man,

Hermaphrodites make their own fun, it's grand,

Hoots juice, there's lots of virgins a'loose,

I am sure you've fixed one to your caboose,

MY VALENTINE (cont.)......

Ah, the old grey mare ain't what she used to be,

I'll dream of growing old disgracefully,

Across the time and centuries,

You'll be the Valentine for me,

I love you to the moon, and beyond,

An endless love affair, it goes on and on........

FIDO.........

Here is my story about a giant dog, Fido,

Once he suspected burglars, way to go,

But I had to protect him, you know,

Maybe Fido needs a dildo!

THIS IS THE WAY……..

My mummy got pulled over today,

My mummy was speeding on the highway,

Mummy did something funny with her mouth,

Now the policeman's headed south,

Yah, mummy, that's the way,

That's how mummy dodged her ticket today!

TIMMY'S TRIPPING.....

This is a sordid little tale,

Cautionary advice did fail,

Timmy got mixed up with the wrong crowd,

Really, Timmy, tripping's not allowed,

Now little Timmy is hallucinating,

Drug squad weren't procrastinating,

Yes, all that sage advice did fail,

Timmy's in drug rehab, sordid tale........

MAIL ORDER!

If I could do some online shopping,

The delivery van here would be stopping,

I would mail order me a man,

Someone sincere to whom I'd hand,

Trust and credibility,

Sensing some sensibility,

Must browse for my mail order man,

Nothing like my long gone husband,

Must do some online shopping,

Here the delivery van would be stopping,

That would be the end of the world, I guess,

If I had someone to trust, no less!

LET'S RIDE.........

This is a tale of long ago..........

We had no seat belts in cars, you know,

So, we grew up to be teens,

 Hitchhiking was our scene,

It was a wonder we all survived,

 Aging baby boomers certainly thrived,

Yes, we said, let's ride with strangers,

 Maybe the world was a lot safer,

We did not consider stranger danger,

Yes, a wonder baby boomers survived,

 Didn't we all kick on and thrive!

WHALE SONG!

We've hunted them to the verge of extinction, you see,

Dead whales can't wave back in the sea,

So much for protection of their species,

Collect the set of dead whales, for you and me,

 Well, great, so much for empathy,

Way to go, humanity!

CLAP TRAP PARTY!

Someone said it was all claptrap,

What, indeed was that?

Why, religion and faith, perhaps,

Or is it a crutch, for some chicks and chaps?

But true love never dies,

I write here, with a smile,

A church is never empty,

We can have a clap trap party,

Faith is quite obligation free,

I keep my eyes on Our Lord, J. C.,

To follow in the path of God,

Believers on their path still trod!

TO THE TUNE: "GRAND OLD FLAG!" (A parody).

Oh, we're grand old farts,

We're high flying farts,

We barrack for shit footy teams,

These days, I've turned to Theology,

All I can say to thee,

Is Jesus and Buddha, so it seems,

Are an excellent team,

Yes, my own team, for thee,

Jesus and Buddha—an excellent team,

But, we're grand old farts,

And we're high flying farts,

We barrack for shit football teams,

Except for Jesus and Buddha, so it seems!

SOUL FOOD!

Here is an ode for each of you,

Prayer is really soul food,

Prayers for each other,

We're all sisters and brothers,

Prayers for our ambitions,

Prayers for good intentions,

To our Lord we are all appealing,

 And of course, we pray in gratitude,

Thank you, Father, for Jesus, and our soul food!

AN EXCELLENT NAME!

As I put pen to paper,

Or tap a keyboard, later?

Oh, Jesus is an excellent name,

Keep our eyes on Jesus, game!

Yes, a forever friend in Jesus, yah!

His rugged cross for us today,

Keep our eyes on Jesus, game,

Oh, Jesus is an excellent name!

ALL THE LIGHT!

This is all about the light,

We cannot see tonight,

But, fear not, my little flock,

It's sun arise, quite a shock,

On earth and heaven above,

Where there's eternal peace of doves,

Yes, we can sense, but cannot see tonight,

Our path to God, all about the light!

THE POCKET BOOK OF..........

Here in a world of books,

I think about a bunch of sooks,

I write my little pocket book,

Being a poet was all it took,

So, that was my little book of verse,

Look forward, never reverse!

****

THE END!

****

17615217R10047

Printed in Great Britain
by Amazon